MY PET

Puppy

Honor Head

Photographs by Jane Burton

**RAINTREE
STECK-VAUGHN
PUBLISHERS**

RSVP

A Harcourt Company

Austin   New York
www.steck-vaughn.com

Published by Raintree Steck-Vaughn Publishers, an imprint of Steck-Vaughn Company.

Editors: Claire Edwards, Erik Greb
Art Director: Max Brinkmann
Designer: Rosamund Saunders
Illustrator: Pauline Bayne

Printed in Singapore

1 2 3 4 5 6 7 8 9 0 LB 03 02 01 00

Library of Congress Cataloging-in-Publication Data

Head, Honor.
  Puppy/Honor Head; photographs by Jane Burton.
    p. cm.—(My pet)
  Summary: Describes the physical characteristics and habits of puppies and tells how to care for them as pets.
    ISBN 0-7398-2885-1 (hardcover)
    ISBN 0-7398-3012-0 (softcover)
    1. Puppies—Juvenile literature. [1. Dogs. 2. Animals—infancy. 3. Pets.] I. Burton, Jane, ill. II. Title.

SF426.5 H423 2000
                              00–027051

Some dogs in this book are shown without collars. This is for photographic purposes only.

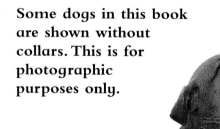

Contents

My Puppy

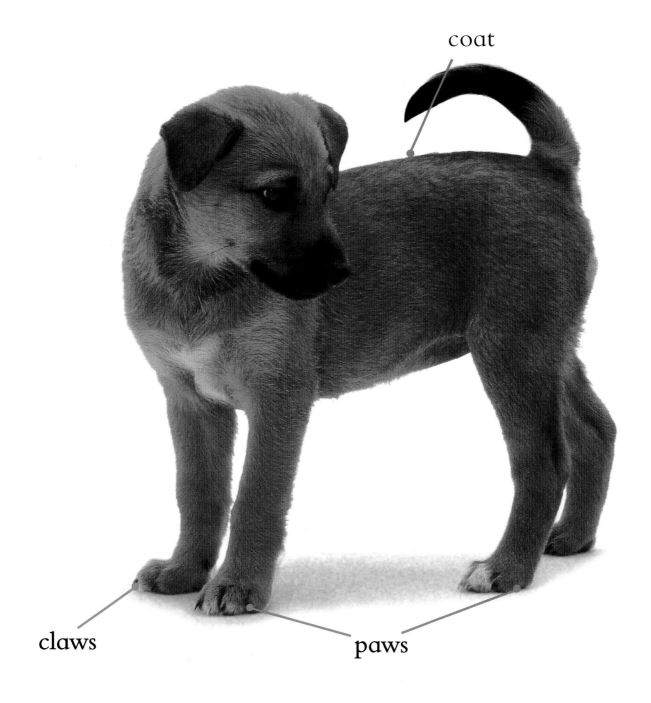

coat

claws

paws

It's fun to have your own pet.

Puppies look sweet and are fun
to play with, but they need
to be looked after carefully.

A puppy needs to be fed
every day and
groomed regularly.
It will also have to be
trained. Most of all,
remember that your
puppy will grow up
and be with you for
a long time.

Young children with
pets should always
work with an adult.
For further notes,
please see page 32.

Dogs come in all shapes and sizes.

Small dogs can be easier to care for than large dogs. They need less space at home and eat less. But they still need plenty of exercise and attention.

Collies, terriers, and dachshunds are different breeds of dogs. They all make good pets. But each breed has its own special needs.

Big dogs can be very strong, and need long walks each day. They can be rough when they play. A big dog could even knock you over.

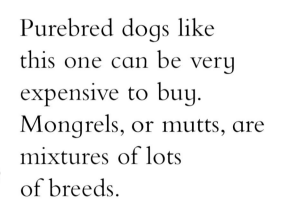

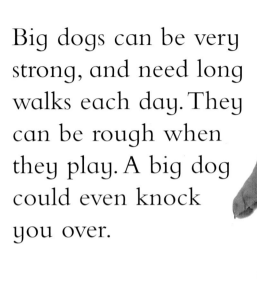

Purebred dogs like this one can be very expensive to buy. Mongrels, or mutts, are mixtures of lots of breeds.

A pregnant dog needs extra care.

A female dog is called a bitch. When she is pregnant, her stomach grows bigger as the puppies grow. You can see the puppies moving inside her. A mother dog needs to be treated very gently.

When a bitch becomes pregnant, her shape changes. Her stomach grows bigger and rounder.

The pregnant mother will look for a cozy, quiet place to have her puppies. A box or basket lined with newspaper and blankets is ideal for her.

You can watch the puppies being born, but do not get too close.

A mother usually has between four and eight puppies, but she may have more. The new puppies can barely crawl.

When puppies are born, they cannot see or hear.

Puppies are born with their eyes and ears closed. They find their way to their mother's milk by smell. Drinking her milk is called suckling.

As the puppies grow older, they will jump all over each other. They squeal and yelp, but they are only playing.

These puppies are one day old. While they are asleep, the mother can stretch her legs and have something to eat.

Puppies need to see a vet when they are four weeks old and may need to be wormed.

The mother licks her puppies to keep them clean. They can be gently stroked now.

Soon the puppies will be old enough to leave their mother.

When a puppy is about eight weeks old, it is old enough to leave its mother. It may be frightened and miss its family. When you take a puppy home, talk to it quietly so that it gets to know your voice.

Puppies sleep a lot. Don't wake a puppy when it is asleep. When it is tired of playing, let it rest.

Your puppy will race and tumble around the house. Make sure there are no wires for it to trip over. Remove dangerous objects such as prickly plants.

Always hold your puppy properly. Put one hand underneath its bottom and the other around its chest. Hold your puppy close to you, but do not squeeze it.

Puppies enjoy playing.

Puppies often pretend to fight each other. They are just playing and won't hurt each other.

Puppies like chewing things, especially when their teeth are growing.

You can play games with your puppy. Throw a ball for it to catch, or play tug of war with a piece of cloth. If your puppy bites you playfully, say "No" in a firm voice.

If you leave your puppy alone, make sure it has toys to play with. This will keep it from being bored or playing with something it should not.

Give your puppy its own toy to play with, such as an old teddy bear.

Make your puppy feel at home.

Find somewhere quiet and warm for your puppy's bed. You can buy a basket from a pet store or make one yourself. Put a blanket inside.

To make a bed for your dog, cut the front from a box and line it with a warm blanket.

Buy special bowls for your puppy – one for food and one for water. Feed it small meals four times a day. Make sure it always has fresh water to drink.

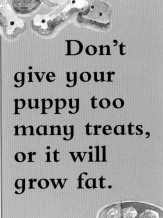

Don't give your puppy too many treats, or it will grow fat.

Your puppy will enjoy bone-shaped chews. These will help to keep its teeth clean and strong. Do not give your puppy cooked or small bones, since these can make it choke. Buy large, uncooked marrow bones from the butcher.

You will need to train your puppy.

Once your puppy has settled in, teach it its name. Stand or sit nearby and call its name. When it comes to you, give it a big hug.

When you feed or play with your puppy, say its name so that it grows used to hearing it.

Your puppy must learn to sit when it is told to do so. Each time your puppy sits, say the word "Sit." Say kind things and hug it when it does as you ask.

Your puppy must be toilet trained. Take it outside after it has eaten, before bed, and when it wakes up. If it sniffs around and looks as if it is going to make a mess, call a grown-up.

Take your puppy to see the vet.

When your puppy is about 12 weeks old, you should take it to the vet. Take it on the leash or in a special dog carrier.

You may want to take your puppy to a vet to be neutered. This will keep your puppy from having unwanted puppies.

The vet will give your puppy a checkup and some shots. She will look at its ears and teeth to make sure your puppy is healthy.

If your puppy is sick, make sure it is kept warm and in a quiet place.

If your puppy has an upset stomach, is very quiet, and doesn't eat, it may need to visit the vet. If your puppy is sick, treat it gently. Make sure it has a bowl of fresh water to drink.

Your puppy needs a walk every day.

You should not let your puppy meet other dogs until it has had all its shots. When your puppy is used to its leash, take it for a walk. Do not pull your puppy by the leash.

All dogs should wear a collar and tag with the owner's name and telephone number on it.

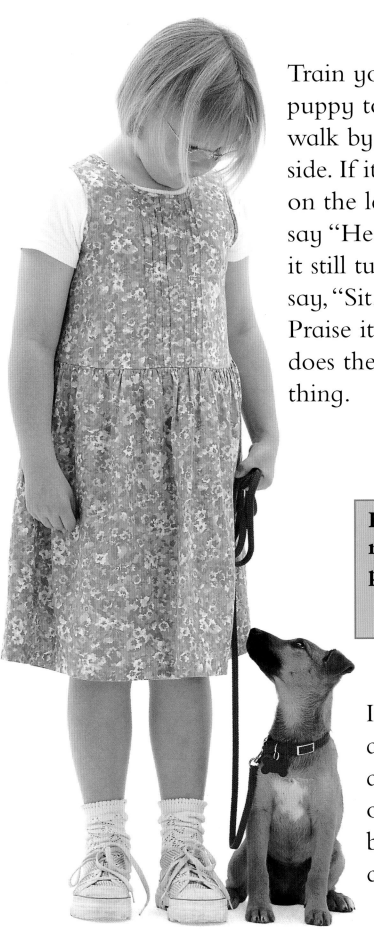

Train your puppy to walk by your side. If it tugs on the leash, say "Heel." If it still tugs, say, "Sit." Praise it when it does the right thing.

If your dog makes a mess, use a scoop and a plastic bag to clean it up.

If you are near farm animals or close to a road, always keep your puppy on the leash. Train it to sit by your side before you cross the road.

Keep your puppy clean.

When you come back from a walk in the rain, or through a muddy field or park, wipe your dog with a towel to keep it clean and dry.

Your puppy will learn to clean itself, but you should brush it for a few minutes every day to help keep its coat healthy. This is called grooming.

Buy a special brush and comb to groom your puppy. Brush the coat gently from the head down to the tail.

If your puppy keeps scratching, it might have fleas. These insects live in its fur. Ask your vet for some flea spray or powder.

How is your puppy feeling?

When your puppy runs to you with its tail in the air and its ears pointed up, it is happy.

When a puppy is unhappy or scared, it keeps its head down, or tucks its tail between its legs. It might need a big hug.

Your puppy may sit up and look at you with its head on one side. This means it is hoping for a game or a treat.

When your puppy crouches with its bottom in the air, it wants to play. It may also wag its tail from side to side.

If a puppy is angry, it crouches down, growls, and shows its teeth. If your puppy looks like this, leave it alone.

Your puppy will soon grow up.

By the time your puppy is about
a year old, it will be a fully grown
dog. Big dogs change a lot as they
grow, but smaller dogs do not
look very different.

As your dog grows older, it will
sleep more and play less. It will
still enjoy being hugged, stroked,
and brushed.

Dogs live for 18 years or more. But, like people, they grow old and die. If your pet is very sick or badly injured, it may also die.

You may feel sad when this happens, but you will be able to look back and remember all the happy times you had together.

Words to Remember

bitch A female dog.

breed A type of dog.

chews Treats made specially for dogs.

coat A dog's fur.

fleas Tiny, biting insects that live in a dog's fur.

groom To brush or comb your dog's coat.

growl The noise a dog makes when it is angry or scared. It makes the noise with its mouth closed.

mongrel A dog that is a mixture of several breeds.

purebred A dog that has been specially bred from other dogs of the same breed.

suckling When a puppy drinks its mother's milk, it is suckling.

treats Special snacks.

vet A doctor for animals.

wormed Treated by the vet to keep an animal from having worms. These could live in its stomach and make it sick.

A newborn puppy.

At three weeks, a puppy likes to sleep a lot.

At eight weeks, a puppy is old enough to leave its mother.

Index

Notes for Parents

A dog will give you and your family a great deal of pleasure, but it is a big responsibility. If you decide to buy a puppy for your child, you will need to ensure that the animal is healthy, happy, and safe. You will have to train and feed your pet, and care for it if it is sick. You will also have to help your child care for the animal until he or she is at least five years old.

Here are some other points to think about before you decide to own a dog:

- A dog can live for about 18 years and can cost a lot of money in food and vet's bills. A dog needs an annual injection and regular worming. An average-sized dog can cost more than $1,000 a year to look after.

- If you work outside the home, do not leave your dog on its own all day. If you have vacations abroad, you will have to pay kennel fees.

- All male and female dogs should be neutered to prevent unwanted litters.

Different breeds of dogs have different temperaments. Some are more excitable than others, so choose your breed carefully. A vet will be able to advise you on which breed is suitable for you:

- Do you have very young or elderly people in the house?

- How often and for how long can you take your dog walking?

- Do you have a yard? Is there a park or open space nearby?

All dogs by law should have a collar and identification tag. Vets can now insert a tiny microchip, the size of a grain of rice, under the dog's skin. This can be scanned to give details of the dog's owners.

This book is only an introduction for young readers. If you have any questions about how to take care of your puppy, you can contact the Humane Society of the U.S., 2100 L Street NW, Washington, DC 20037.